T0209746

KNOWLEDGE

— OF THE —

HOUR

TORATI

authorHOUSE®

AuthorHouse™
1663 Liberty Drive
Bloomington, IN 47403
www.authorhouse.com
Phone: 1 (800) 839-8640

Published by AuthorHouse 08/27/2019

Scripture quotations marked NIV are taken from the Holy Bible, New International Version®. NIV®. Copyright © 1973, 1978, 1984 by International Bible Society. Used by permission of Zondervan. All rights reserved. [Biblica]

ISBN: 978-1-7283-2479-1 (sc)
ISBN: 978-1-7283-2478-4 (e)

In this book, I recognize the company and prayers of my brothers and sisters Dairohim, Abeli, Aroni, Samuel, Seti, Veronika, Marieli-Raeli, Mariam-Damarieli, Ezrali, Luka, and Dieu-Merci.

CHAPTER 1

THE SWORD OF SALVATION

Beloved brethren and believers of Jesus Christ in the whole world, in righteousness and in truth, may the peace of the Lord be with you all. To all of you who have not known Jesus Christ or were not taught to believe in Almighty God who created you, receive the peace and blessings of the foundation of salvation in your hearts.

Since the foundation of the universe was laid, the whole world has been under the leadership of the law and commandments of the Lord God, the Creator of all, through the light that led His creation, Adam, before he fell into sin. They saw the glory of God and lived His holiness. When they were tried by the old serpent, in the mystery of the heavens, this one called Satan, who is also Lucifer, the father of all evil, they bore death in them, and they chased away the initial glory that was in them. However, the Lord did not abandon them. He kept on being with them through His grace, and they kept being taught the secrets of times and seasons of the universe. They were taught the way to give the Lord thanksgiving offerings and burned sacrifices so as to give back respect and glory to God by worshipping Him during their time on earth.

The evil one, Lucifer, in his evilness, was thrown into the universe to bring woe unto the world and all those who live in it. He even waged war on the holy ones of God. He misled many of them and destroyed the times and seasons that the Lord God Almighty had put in place. This evil one removed them from glory and put them into eternal corruption.

Today, there are not many who are righteous, even though they fellowship in church. Instead, many are ruled by hypocrisy and injustice

1

in their hearts. The Lord Almighty God used to mind humans so much that the heavens served them and mighty angels came down to inform them about what the Lord Almighty intended to do. But many human beings have strayed for lack of knowledge and have not cared to mind the glorious voice (Hosea 4:6–12). He sent prophets and messengers to remind people what they were taught by the Lord God, their Father. Many did not obey or respect them; instead, they killed them and threw them in prisons. Others were stoned, and still others were burned. Even when He sent Jesus Christ, they did not leave Him alone, for they pretended to be holier than the Son of God. They persecuted and even crucified Him to death. Later, He ascended to God. Jesus Christ left a large army and a large group of disciples, elders, and priests to restore His righteousness to the universe. They too were humiliated, beaten badly, and even killed. And the righteousness departed again.

Even though all this happened, the Almighty still loves the world, and He is on the way together with Jesus Christ to bring the final judgment to the world. Behold, Satan and his followers do not sleep day and night as they plan strategies to come and mislead the followers of Jesus Christ so that there is not a single righteous one in the universe. Despite this, Almighty God has also kept sending other messengers, prophets, and priests so that they continue to establish an awakening, startle human beings, and teach them the righteousness that comes from the Lord. They also come to lead human beings to the true way of Jesus Christ so that the Father's kingdom can come down to earth, people can be saved, and believers get to enjoy the fruits of the land.

Let us say the world has lost righteousness. This is the time of the Lord to restore His righteousness to the way of Jesus Christ in the whole universe. Read Jesus Christ's words in Luke 12:2–5. The followers of the devil and their father, Satan, sat down and discussed which ways they could use to remove the manifestation of the glory of Jesus Christ from the universe after He ascended to heaven and left His disciples on the work of the gospel on earth. These evil ones empowered themselves and killed all the disciples except that beloved one, John, who was locked away on Patmos Island, where he was enabled to get the final revelation and the occurrences of this world today.

The believers of Jesus Christ kept encouraging each other to believe in Him in secret, and they multiplied a lot, even though the evil ones kept planning ways to finish them. The evil ones did not manage to finish them since they did not have any powers over human beings except when God of all heaven let them. He, the Father, is the ruler of heaven and earth and all that is in them. When the children of the evil Lucifer (Satan) and his devils saw that they could not manage, they sat down in their grand six-day summit, planning how to destroy the traditional account and order of hours, days, months, and years so that the believers in the world could not understand the destructive politics and the way it was planned. Nor could they know the way that the world was going or the way it used to be.

In waiting for their kingdom (the primitive one—world order) to get a good chance to mislead many and for the spiritual universe not to recognize itself, they used the name of our Lord Jesus Christ and betrayed it in the mystery of the spirit. They also blindfolded the believers so that they could not see where they were headed. When those evil ones met, it became clear that they were led by their father, Satan, and his devils in changing the naming of days and months as well as the count of hours, months, and years. They also planned how to justify philosophically and scientifically their evil deeds.

Let us read about the changes in the calendar, for that is where the Antichrist infiltrated the body of Christ, the temple of God.

CHAPTER 2

THE DISTORTION OF THE CALENDAR

When the ten kings came together, they changed the days of the year, the months, the weeks, and the hours. For when they followed the Bible, they discovered that it showed clearly in the books of Revelation, John, Daniel, and the prophets when they speak of 1,260 days (or forty-two months) that a month has thirty days and a year has 360 days. (Read Revelation 11:2–3 and 12:6 and Daniel 12:11.) But those kings of the world decided to add six different days for themselves and the glory of Almighty God in a normal year for human beings. Also, in several months, they added one extra day (in the first, third, fifth, seventh, eighth, tenth, and twelfth months), and in their second month, they reduced it by one day in years A, B, and C. And in the liturgical year, they gave it twenty-nine days once a year after three years. This is the fourth year.

You will find that there are three years with 365 days followed by one year with 366 days. All of this is because of their worship of their female god called the queen of the heavens, for whom they burned frankincense, as was the custom with their fathers to their gods.

Regarding the idol that represents this female god, they gave her the name Mary, the mother of Jesus Christ, while showing how she cared for her baby. Although it's not true, they put a halo around her head like it's a crown. They established legions of Mary in worshipping this queen of the heavens and even mention her in their prayers. They pray in the rosary, saying that Mary, the mother of Jesus Christ, appeared to them and taught them that. But it's not true. Understand one matter: Mary, the mother of

Jesus Christ, is not the queen of heaven, and it is not good when you pray in front of an idol and ask Mary to intercede for you with her son, Jesus Christ. It is not okay. However, it will be good when you show respect to Mary as a woman who cooperated with the Holy Spirit of God to bear Jesus Christ, who is the Living God, and manifested God the Creator of all heavens and earth and all that is in them.

They also left some months in their normal thirty days, and these are the fourth, sixth, ninth, and eleventh months. It is a blatant lie that there are 365 and a quarter days in a year, for since heaven and earth were created, there has never been a quarter day with only six hours. In spiritual realms, one hour has 120 seconds, and a day has twelve hours with two timings—night and day—in angelic timing. Yet they spoiled them and made the third spiritual month to be the zero month to them. Three equals zero so that they could fool everyone in every nation. Although 9=0=6 has value in the Spirit, it has no value in the world. This is the translation of the distortion of the year. You will find that there are days that differ and that when you put them together, their value is 0, either 2 or 4 and rarely 6 and 9. It appears once with 2 and 4 since they are the signs that the devil hides in using the number 8.

Days were arranged under the leadership of Constantine the Great on March 7, 321, after Jesus Christ ascended to heaven, in the town of Nicaea. They had met to discuss that there were ten kings from the ten great nations of old times: Germany, Italy, France, Portugal, England, Spain, Switzerland, Heruli, Austria, and Vorgato. These are the ones who were led by their lord, Satan, and the devil to change the genuine names of days, months, seasons, and times of this universe.[1] And those ten kings are represented by the ten tribes that rule as cardinals in Rome (Revelations 17:12).

When you read the Bible, in Luke 1:26–31, you will hear it say that Mary was told by the angel that she would conceive and bear Jesus Christ, and it was the sixth month. That sixth month was in the sixth year as per the laws that were given to Moses and is also the sixth month of the pregnancy of Elizabeth, the sister of Mary. Therefore, know very well that when you read from Luke 1:2a–31, you will clearly understand this. And

---

[1] https://www.historychannel.com.au/this-day-in-history/constantine-decrees-sun-day-as-day-of-rest/.

all that became the zero year in spiritual terms, because, as now, there is not a single person who lives it except that one who was revealed to us by the Great Lord God. These ones took the day that Jesus Christ was born on the thirtieth of Siwani month in the year 6 toward the year 5, and they said that this day was called December 30, which is the twelfth month, in the year 0. Zero means there is nothing that is or came before and this is the beginning, or maybe let us say it is the silence of death and the start of a new life. That is the reason for 0 even when they say 00:00, meaning we bury the past and start afresh in the night while others sleep so that they will not be able to know what we did. They will find that we have already organized, and they will only visit what we give them. That is why you as a Christian should not sleep like the dead. Then, 23h is 0h since 24h is as 23h because 2+4=6 for man and 2×3=6 for man, but 2+4=2+1=3 becomes a mystery in spirituality, since 4=1 in spiritual settings. Yet when they remove that 1, it remains 23 so that it is hidden in the foolishness of worshipping Satan in the number 6. They made it the start of their day, the children of the devil and their Satan. That is why every hour was moved from His glory and put in the sign of 6 to bring a difference. The second hour of the day, they put as 8 and the third hour as 9. The fourth hour is 10, the fifth hour 11, the sixth hour 12. The first hour is 7, or the seventh hour is 1, and the seventh hour is also 13. When you get the difference, every time, you will find that you get 6, whether going forward or backward.

They argued among themselves, saying that because this Jesus Christ is the Great King of all believers in the world, they know certainly that He is the Son of the Living God, and so we should exalt our god to manifest in the light of the sun on December 25 every year and make it a celebration for all the people in the world, announcing that it is the day that Jesus Christ was born so that we can mislead His believers. They all agreed, and it was so. And so, it became a holiday to exalt their god Mithra, a resident of Iran, an Iranian, and also Dionisa Bakkus, the only son of the god Jupiter, a resident of Greece. And so they called this day Noël, meaning there is no God, and they will be conquered by those two gods, Mithra and Dionisa. When you look, there is an ë with two dots, meaning two kings (el = God, and *no* as a denying prefix). It is also the day they exalt the god Jupiter, praising him and saying Father Noël, who is the father who begot

Noël. Sometimes, they call it X-mass, meaning the remembering of those ten kings who were at the meeting table. They also said it should be called "Chrissmass," meaning an assembly of the table of Chriss, meaning kings.

IGNORANCE

We mention this day of Christmas because many people think that it is an important day that they celebrate to fulfil the scripture of the great day of the birth of the Great Redeemer of the universe, Jesus Christ. That is not true, for it is a great corruption for all those who celebrate it because they support the worldly kings and worship their gods. Among the gods of the worldly kings, there are many who compared themselves to Jesus Christ, but they did not fulfil their intentions. They wanted their names to be higher than the name of Jesus Christ, but they could not manage. Many of them are from Asia and Europe as well as Egypt.

X-MASS NA NOËL

The word *Chrissmass* means the worship of kings, an assembly of kings, the table of kings or X-Mass, meaning the assembly of ten. That is the seating of the ten representatives we mentioned earlier. In their mystery, they mentioned that Chrissmass was set up by an assembly of Christian believers, yet it is the agreement of ten kings in changing the calendar of the world and bestowing one religious king who will be ruling and owning the others. And they called him the "representative father," meaning the pope. Many people after Christ and those before Him looked at prophecies about the coming of Christ and all that was prophesied, and they desired to take the praise of the Lord and give themselves His glorious name.

THE TRUTH SHOULD SET YOU FREE

No-ël—no = not, el=god—shows clearly that it is not the day to praise Jesus Christ God; rather, it is a day of putting oneself in the chains of worldly gods. All of their gods burned and were destroyed, yet they are ashamed to exalt Jesus Christ, who was resurrected. They keep fearing and exalting the worldlings. Do not join the stupid fools, the way the members of the Catholic denomination do. It is a holiday for those who are ruled by Romans, who used to celebrate the holiday of the sun, for to them, the light was their king. They called it the holiday of the god of the sun. They believed that the sun is a god. That time, the king Mithra, who was Iranian, was born by witchcraft power without a father and through a virgin girl, one of the Romans, so that this becomes his day to be worshipped. They bore him like that so that he bore the image of Christ, the Redeemer of the world. This is the one who is celebrated on December 25 every year. Among the many bishops in the world and the many pastors who are hypocrites of the Roman churches, Greece and Germany follow the celebration of Chrissmass and Noël as well as their day of the Passover, which is not compatible with the plan of the Lord God Almighty. They put it so that it would exalt their other gods, who were also born on December 25, 62, died in the third month toward the end, and were resurrected in the fourth month in the beginning. They appeared in the season of disturbing people, and this is the first virus that appeared in the form of a vampire called Adoris, the god of the tribe of Syria. This Adonis (Adoris) has very many followers in the world who worship him in many churches. There is also the god Dionysus/Bacchus, the only son of the god Jupiter, whom they gave a dwelling on a planet called Jupiter. He also was born the same day, December 25, and he took the name of the first and the last as the alpha and omega. When he died, he descended into hell and was imprisoned. There appeared an angel of darkness with that name, and he used his image to mislead the nations that he resurrected and called himself that name. The heavens opened, and the fire licked the angel of darkness. Many Gentiles were saved, and others announced that he was taken in death. This one is of Greek origin.

There is also Attis, the god of Tigris origin, where his headquarters are. He was born to a virgin named Nana and was killed on March 24 under a pine tree. Through his blood, he was called the redeemer whenever it fell and dried up. There was a lot of great magic that happened that day. He amazed people with his life and his magic. O children of God, do not forget what the Lord God Almighty did for you in Egypt. Even the Pharaoh's magicians who were doing miracles for him got saved.

CHAPTER 3

THE EGYPTIAN CHURCH COULD PERFORM MIRACLES

We all know that Pharaoh was a believer, but the Lord God of Moses proved to him for many years that Egyptian belief was nothing more than idolatry. We all know that the prophets of Baal were believers, but Elijah proved to them all that God exists, and He is different from what we are seeing today. When a so-called man of God does a "miracle," many of you call him a prophet. Stop your blasphemies. Take time to read the following scriptures from the Torah, the book of Exodus. God cannot be limited by time or space. All those who have been initiated can perform some type of miracle but not as Moses or any other true prophet of God did.

The LORD said to Moses, "See, I've made you like God to Pharaoh, and your brother Aaron will be your prophet. You will say everything that I command you, and your brother Aaron will tell Pharaoh to let the Israelites out of his land. But I'll make Pharaoh stubborn, and I'll perform many of my signs and amazing acts in the land of Egypt. When Pharaoh refuses to listen to you, then I'll act against Egypt and I'll bring my people the Israelites out of the land of Egypt in military formation by momentous events of justice. The Egyptians will come to know that I am the LORD when I act against Egypt and bring the Israelites out from among them. Moses and Aaron did just as the Lord commanded them. Moses was eighty years old, and Aaron was eighty-three when they spoke to Pharaoh. (Exodus 7:1–7)

TURNING RODS INTO SNAKES

The LORD said to Moses and Aaron, "When Pharaoh says to you, 'Do one of your amazing acts,' then say to Aaron, 'Take your shepherd's rod and throw it down in front of Pharaoh, and it will turn into a cobra.'"

So Moses and Aaron went to Pharaoh and did just as the LORD commanded. Aaron threw down his shepherd's rod in front of Pharaoh and his officials, and it turned into a cobra. Then Pharaoh called together his wise men and wizards, and Egypt's religious experts did the same thing by using their secret knowledge. Each one threw down his rod, and they turned into cobras. But then Aaron's rod swallowed up each of their rods. However, Pharaoh remained stubborn. He wouldn't listen to them, just as the LORD had said. (Exodus 7:8–13)

WATER INTO BLOOD

Then the LORD said to Moses, "Pharaoh is stubborn. He still refuses to let the people go. Go to Pharaoh in the morning. As he is going out to the water, make sure you stand at the bank of the Nile River so you will run into him. Bring along the shepherd's rod that turned into a snake. Say to him, The LORD, the Hebrews' God, has sent me to you with this message: Let my people go so that they can worship me in the desert. Up to now you still haven't listened. This is what the LORD says: By this, you will know that I am the LORD. I'm now going to hit the water of the Nile River with this rod in my hand, and it will turn into blood. The fish in the Nile is going to die, the Nile will stink, and the Egyptians won't be able to drink water from the Nile."

The Lord said to Moses, "Say to Aaron, 'Take your shepherd's rod and stretch out your hand over Egypt's waters—over their rivers, their canals, their marshes, and all their bodies of water—so that they turn into blood. There will be blood all over the land of Egypt, even in wooden and stone containers.'"

Moses and Aaron did just as the Lord commanded. He raised the shepherd's rod and hit the water in the Nile in front of Pharaoh and his officials, and all the water in the Nile turned into blood. The fish in the Nile died, and the Nile began to stink so that the Egyptians couldn't drink water from the Nile. There was blood all over the land of Egypt. But the Egyptian religious experts did the same thing with their secret knowledge. As a result, Pharaoh remained stubborn, and he wouldn't listen to them, just as the Lord had said. Pharaoh turned and went back to his palace. He wasn't impressed even by this. Meanwhile, all the Egyptians had to dig for drinking water along the banks of the Nile River, because they couldn't drink the water of the Nile itself. Seven days went by after the Lord had struck the Nile River. (Exodus 7:14–25)

INVASION OF FROGS

Then the Lord said to Moses, "Go to Pharaoh and tell him: This is what the Lord says: Let my people go so that they can worship me. If you refuse to let them go, then I'll send a plague of frogs over your whole country. The Nile will overflow with frogs. They'll get into your palace, into your bedroom and onto your bed, into your officials' houses, and among all your people, and even into your ovens and bread pans. The frogs will crawl up on you, your people, and all your officials. And the Lord said to Moses, "Tell Aaron, 'Stretch out your hand with your shepherd's rod over the rivers, the canals, and the marshes, and make the frogs crawl up all over the land of Egypt.'" So Aaron stretched out his hand over the waters of Egypt. The frogs crawled up and covered the land of Egypt. However, the Egyptian religious experts were able to do the same thing by their secret knowledge. They too made frogs crawl up onto the land of Egypt.

Then Pharaoh called for Moses and Aaron, and said, "If you pray to the LORD to get rid of the frogs from me and my people, then I'll let the people go so that they can offer sacrifices to the LORD."

Moses said to Pharaoh, "Have it your way. When should I pray for you and your officials and your people to remove the frogs from your houses, courtyards, and fields? They'll stay only in the Nile."

Pharaoh said, "Tomorrow!"

Moses said, "Just as you say! That way you will know that there is no one like the LORD our God. The frogs will leave you, your houses, your officials, and your people. They'll stay only in the Nile." After Moses and Aaron had left Pharaoh, Moses cried out to the LORD about the frogs that the LORD had brought on Pharaoh. The LORD did as Moses asked. The frogs died inside the houses, out in the yards, and in the fields. They gathered them together in big piles, and the land began to stink. But when Pharaoh saw that the disaster was over, he became stubborn again and wouldn't listen to them, just as the LORD had said. (Exodus 8:1–14)

SWARMING LICE

Then the LORD said to Moses, "Tell Aaron, 'Stretch out your shepherd's rod and hit the land's dirt so that lice appear in the whole land of Egypt.'" They did this. Aaron stretched out his hand with his shepherd's rod, hit the land's dirt, and lice appeared on both people and animals.

All the land's dirt turned into lice throughout the whole land of Egypt.

The religious experts tried to produce lice by their secret knowledge, but they weren't able to do it. There were lice on people and animals. The religious experts said to Pharaoh, "This is something only God could do!" But Pharaoh was stubborn, and he wouldn't listen to them, just as the LORD had said. (Exodus 8:15–19)

INSECTS FILL EGYPT

The LORD said to Moses, "Get up early in the morning and confront Pharaoh as he goes out to the water. Say to him, this is what the LORD says: Let my people go so that they can worship me. If you refuse to let my people go, I'll send swarms of insects on you, your officials, your people, and your houses. All Egyptian houses will be filled with swarms of insects and also the ground that they cover. But on that day I'll set apart the land of Goshen, where my people live. No swarms of insects will come there so you will know that I, the LORD, am in this land. I'll put a barrier between my people and your people. This sign will happen tomorrow." The LORD did this. Great swarms of insects came into the houses of Pharaoh and his officials and into the whole land of Egypt. The land was ruined by the insects.

Then Pharaoh called in Moses and Aaron and said, "Go, offer sacrifices to your God within the land."

Moses replied, "It wouldn't be right to do that, because the sacrifices that we offer to the LORD our God will offend Egyptians. If we openly offer sacrifices that offend Egyptians, won't they stone us to death? We need to go for a three-day journey into the desert to offer sacrifices to the LORD our God as he has ordered us."

So Pharaoh said, "I'll let you go to offer sacrifices to the LORD your God in the desert, provided you don't go too far away and you pray for me."

Moses said, "I'll leave you now, and I'll pray to the LORD. Tomorrow the swarms of insects will leave Pharaoh, his officials, and his people. Just don't let Pharaoh lie to us again and not let the people go to offer sacrifices to the LORD."

So Moses left Pharaoh and prayed to the LORD. The LORD did as Moses asked and removed the swarms of insects from Pharaoh, from his officials, and from his people. Not one insect remained. But Pharaoh was stubborn once again, and he wouldn't let the people go. (Exodus 8:20–30)

ANIMALS SICK AND DYING

Then the LORD said to Moses, "Go to Pharaoh and say to him, This is what the LORD, the Hebrews' God, says: Let my people go so that they can worship me. If you refuse to let them go and you continue to hold them back, the LORD will send a very deadly disease on your livestock in the field: on horses, donkeys, camels, cattle, and flocks. But the LORD will distinguish Israel's livestock from Egypt's livestock so that not one that belongs to the Israelites will die." The LORD set a time and said, "Tomorrow the LORD will do this in the land." And the next day the LORD did it. All of the Egyptian livestock died, but not one animal that belonged to the Israelites died. Pharaoh asked around and found out that not one of Israel's livestock had died. But Pharaoh was stubborn, and he wouldn't let the people go. (Exodus 9:1–7)

SKIN SORES AND BLISTERS

Then the LORD said to Moses and Aaron, "Take handfuls of ashes from a furnace and have Moses throw it up in the air in front of Pharaoh. The ashes will turn to soot over the whole land of Egypt. It will cause skin sores that will break out in blisters on people and animals in the whole land of Egypt." So they took ashes from the furnace, and they stood in front of Pharaoh. Moses threw the ash up in the air, and it caused skin sores and blisters to break out on people and animals. The religious experts couldn't stand up to Moses because of the skin sores, because there were skin sores on the religious experts as well as on all the Egyptians. But the LORD made Pharaoh stubborn, and Pharaoh wouldn't listen to them, just as the LORD had said to Moses. (Exodus 9:8–12)

HAIL AND THUNDER

Then the LORD said to Moses, "Get up early in the morning and confront Pharaoh. Say to him, this is what the LORD, the God of the Hebrews, says: Let my people go so that they can worship me. This time I'm going to send all my plagues on you, your officials, and your people so that you will know that there is no one like me in the whole world. By now I could have used my power to strike you and your people with a deadly disease so that you would have disappeared from the earth. But I've left you standing for this reason: in order to show you my power and in order to make my name known in the whole world. You are still abusing your power against my people, and you refuse to let them go. Tomorrow at this time I'll cause the heaviest hail to fall on Egypt that has ever fallen from the day Egypt was founded until now. So bring under shelter your livestock and all that belongs to you that is out in the open. Every person or animal that is out in the open field and isn't brought inside will die when the hail rains down on them." Some of Pharaoh's officials who took the LORD's word seriously rushed to bring their servants and livestock inside for shelter. Others who didn't take the LORD's word to the heart left their servants and livestock out in the open field.

The LORD said to Moses, "Raise your hand toward the sky so that hail will fall on the whole land of Egypt, on people and animals and all the grain in the fields in the land of Egypt." Then Moses raised his shepherd's rod toward the sky, and the LORD sent thunder and hail, and lightning struck the earth. The LORD rained hail on the land of Egypt. The hail and the lightning flashing in the middle of the hail were so severe that there had been nothing like it in the entire land of Egypt since it first became a nation. The hail beat down everything that was in the open field throughout the entire land of Egypt, both people and animals. The hail also beat down all the grain in the fields, and it shattered every tree out in the field. The only place where hail didn't fall was in the land of Goshen where the Israelites lived.

Then Pharaoh sent for Moses and Aaron and said to them, "This time I've sinned. The LORD is right, and I and my people are wrong. Pray to the LORD! Enough of God's thunder and hail! I'm going to let you go. You don't need to stay here any longer."

Moses said to him, "As soon as I've left the city, I'll spread out my hands to the LORD. Then the thunder and the hail will stop and won't return so that you will know that the earth belongs to the LORD. But I know that you and your officials still don't take the LORD God seriously." (Now the flax and the barley were destroyed because the barley had ears of grain and the flax had buds. But both durum and spelt wheat weren't ruined, because they hadn't come up.) Moses left Pharaoh and the city and spread out his hands to the LORD. Then the thunder and the hail stopped, and the rain stopped pouring down on the earth. But when Pharaoh saw that the rain, hail, and thunder had stopped, he sinned again. Pharaoh and his officials became stubborn. Because of his stubbornness, Pharaoh refused to let the Israelites go, just as the LORD had told Moses. (Exodus 9:13–35)

INVASION OF LOCUSTS

Then the LORD said to Moses, "Go to Pharaoh. I've made him and his officials stubborn so that I can show them my signs and so that you can tell your children and grandchildren how I overpowered the Egyptians with the signs I did among them. You will know that I am the LORD."

So Moses and Aaron went to Pharaoh and said to him, "This is what the LORD, the Hebrews' God, says: How long will you refuse to respect me? Let my people go so that they can worship me. Otherwise, if you refuse to let my people go, I'm going to bring locusts into your country tomorrow. They will cover the landscape so that you won't be able to see the ground. They will eat the last bit of vegetation that was left after the hail. They will eat all your trees growing in the fields. The locusts will fill your houses and all your officials' houses and all the Egyptians' houses. Your parents and even your grandparents have never seen anything like it during their entire lifetimes in this fertile land." Then Moses turned and left Pharaoh.

Pharaoh's officials said to him, "How long will this man trap us in a corner like this? Let the people go so that they can worship the LORD their God. Don't you get it? Egypt is being destroyed!"

So Moses and Aaron were brought back to Pharaoh, and he said to them, "Go! Worship the LORD your God! But who exactly is going with you?"

Moses said, "We'll go with our young and old, with our sons and daughters, and with our flocks and herds, because we all must observe the LORD's festival."

Pharaoh said to them, "Yes, the LORD will be with you, all right, especially if I let your children go with you!

Obviously, you are plotting some evil scheme. No way! Only your men can go and worship the LORD because that's what you asked for." Then Pharaoh had them chased out of his presence.

Then the LORD said to Moses: "Stretch out your hand over the land of Egypt so that the locusts will swarm over the land of Egypt and eat all of the land's grain and everything that the hail left." So Moses stretched out his shepherd's rod over the land of Egypt, and the LORD made an east wind blow over the land all that day and all that night. When morning came, the east wind had carried in the locusts. The locusts swarmed over the whole land of Egypt and settled on the whole country. Such a huge swarming of locusts had never happened before and would never happen ever again. They covered the whole landscape so that the land turned black with them. They ate all of the land's grain and all of the orchards' fruit that the hail had left. Nothing green was left in an orchard or in any grain field in the whole land of Egypt.

Pharaoh called urgently for Moses and Aaron and said, "I've sinned against the LORD your God and against you. Please, forgive my sin this time. Pray to the LORD your God just to take this deathly disaster away from me."

So Moses left Pharaoh and prayed to the LORD. The LORD turned the wind into a very strong west wind that lifted the locusts and drove them into the Red Sea. Not a single locust was left in the whole country of Egypt. But the LORD made Pharaoh stubborn so that he wouldn't let the Israelites go. (Exodus 10:1–20)

DARKNESS COVERS EGYPT

Then the LORD said to Moses, "Raise your hand toward the sky so that darkness spreads over the land of Egypt, a darkness that you can feel." So Moses raised his hand toward the sky, and intense darkness fell on the whole land of Egypt for three days. People couldn't see each other, and they couldn't go anywhere for three days. But the Israelites all had light where they lived.

Then Pharaoh called Moses and said, "Go! Worship the Lord! Only your flocks and herds need to stay behind. Even your children can go with you."

But Moses said, "You need to let us have sacrificed and entirely burned offerings to present to the Lord our God. So our livestock must go with us. Not one animal can be left behind. We'll need some of them for worshipping the Lord our God. We won't know which to use to worship the Lord until we get there."

But the Lord made Pharaoh stubborn so that he wasn't willing to let them go. Pharaoh said to him, "Get out of here! Make sure you never see my face again, because the next time you see my face you will die."

Moses said, "You've said it! I'll never see your face again!" (Exodus 10:21–29)

GOD ANNOUNCES THE FINAL DISASTER

The Lord said to Moses, "I'll bring one more disaster on Pharaoh and on Egypt. After that, he'll let you go from here. In fact, when he lets you go, he'll eagerly chase you out of here. Tell every man to ask his neighbor and every woman to ask her neighbor for all their silver and gold jewellery." The Lord made sure that the Egyptians were kind to the Hebrew people. In addition, Pharaoh's officials and the Egyptian people even came to honor Moses as a great and important man in the land.

Moses said, "This is what the Lord says: At midnight I'll go throughout Egypt. Every oldest child in the land of Egypt will die, from the oldest child of Pharaoh who sits on his throne to the oldest child of the servant woman by the millstones, and all the first offspring of the animals. Then a terrible cry of agony will echo through the whole land of Egypt unlike any heard before or that ever will be again. But as for the Israelites, not even a dog will growl at them, at the people, or at their animals. By this, you will know that the LORD makes a distinction between Egypt and Israel. Then all your officials will come down to me, bow to me, and say, 'Get out, you and all your followers!' After that, I'll leave." Then Moses, furious, left Pharaoh.

The LORD said to Moses, "Pharaoh won't listen to you so that I can perform even more amazing acts in the land of Egypt." Now Moses and Aaron did all these amazing acts in front of Pharaoh, but the LORD made Pharaoh stubborn so that he didn't let the Israelites go from his land. (Exodus 11:1–9)

DEATH OF EGYPT'S OLDEST CHILDREN

At midnight the LORD struck down all the first offspring in the land of Egypt, from the oldest child of Pharaoh sitting on his throne to the oldest child of the prisoner in jail, and all the first offspring of the animals. When Pharaoh, all his officials, and all the Egyptians got up that night, a terrible cry of agony rang out across Egypt because every house had someone in it who had died. Then Pharaoh called Moses and Aaron that night and said, "Get up! Get away from my people, both you and the Israelites! Go! Worship the LORD, as you said! You can even take your flocks and herds, as you asked. Just go! And bring a blessing on me as well!" (Exodus 12:29–32)

Osiris and Horus are gods of Egyptian origin. They are twins born on December 29. Osiris grew more powerful than the other so that he died and rose again, and his betrayer (like Judas) was Tifeni. This Osiris died an intentional death, and after two days and eight hours, he was alive again. Surprisingly, he had a decomposed body and had been burned alive. His death was intentional so as to be exalted by men. December 26 is the main day for those kings to offer different gifts among themselves, the kings of the whole world, to give unleavened and baked bread and wheat flour and turkey meat. And that is why all the decorations of Christmas have meaning; it's a mystery of the message to the kings of the earth. There is Sederi, which has its meaning, and lights with changing colors as well as green leaves and banana leaves, sculptures in the form of people, stars, idols in the form of angels, statues in the form of cows and sheep, Christmas writings and the Noël to praise that day, Noël's father's image, and many unrecognizable signs. O mankind who believe in Jesus Christ, we are invited to follow *the true way of Jesus Christ*, and neither should you look forward to celebrating the feast day of devil, worshipping pagan gods. The true way of *Jesus Christ* is the one with eternal life. Save your life, and do not be fooled.

CHAPTER 4

THE PROPHET MUHAMMAD TRIED TO CHANGE THE SYSTEM

These churches, temples, synagogues, and mosques you attend today are hell-bent on misleading many to lose their eternal lives. Others are followers of the devil, and some are greedy shepherds in the politics of destruction for their members. Despite this, God is merciful and with great love. He asks us in His mercy through the encouragement of His chosen, before the holy war, that we should change the system and our direction. We should stop evil and act rightly, so we can turn back to Him, and He will hold us by the hand. Despite this, God Almighty did not get tired. Looking through the universe, He saw many believers were fearful and worried. Then in the year following the seasons of men (an account of men or the deceitful calendar), because of His justice, He chose a brave boy in the nation of Asia called Muhammad, who received excellent training from Almighty God and His archangels. He learned about the true way of Jesus Christ.

> Muhammad, age 12, accompanied his uncle Abu Talib during trading journeys to Syria. In one of them, his prophetic status was discovered by Bahira, a Christian monk of Busra al-Sham (southern Syria), who, after taking one look at Muhammad, pulled off his shirt to reveal the "seal of prophecy" (*khatam an-nubuwwah*) between Muhammad's shoulder blades that the monk recognized from ancient manuscripts. Ahmad Ibn Yahya

al-Baladhuri (died 892), one of the most eminent Middle
Eastern historians of his age, tells the following story
in his *Ansab al-A shraf* ("Genealogies of the Nobles"):
When the Prophet of God had reached the age of twelve,
Abu Talib once had to depart to Syria for trade. The
Prophet of God had a close bond with him ... Then
one of the learned monks, whom they called "Bahira,"
saw him while a cloud gave him shade. He said to Abu
Talib: 'how is he related to you?' He answered: "he is
my nephew." He said: 'did you not see how the cloud
gives him shade and moves with him?' By God, he is a
noble prophet and I reckon that he is the one who was
announced by Jesus."

He urged people to return to the Almighty God. And
many of the people of the world obeyed and respected
him, but this young man saw that many believers were
being killed for confessing the name of Jesus Christ, he
also feared for his life. So, he started teaching people to
obey the Almighty God and his prophet, (Jesus Christ).
And kings when they heard him and invited him to be
interrogated: "Which God and his prophet do you speak
of?" He testified to them about Jesus Christ (Whom he
called the Prophet of God). They told him: "If you do that
again, you will also be killed."

Then the Lord God Almighty said to him the following words. Read
Surath Al Maidah 5:54–56 54:

O you who believe; whoever leaves his religion among you,
then soon Allah (the Almighty God) will bring people
whom He will love and they will love him; humble with
fellow Muslims and stern towards the non-believers. They
will fight for the religion of Allah they will not be afraid
of the reproaches of those who blame them. That is the
bounty of Allah; gives whomever he pleases. And Allah
is all-Encompassing and Knowing. Your friend especially

that who praise intent is Allah and His Messenger and the believers who perform prayer and give alms; and the fact that they submit. And whoever befriends Allah and His Messenger and those who believe people will qualify for the party of Allah are they who will win ...

In this ayah (verse), Allah (God) emphasizes His mighty ability and states that whoever reverts from supporting His religion and establishing His law, then He will replace them with whoever is better, mightier, and more righteous in Allah's religion and law. He says that those who had a chance to read the Koran are to understand that Prophet Muhammad had been taught the Torah and the gospel. When he saw that he was loved by many and already had many believers, he decided to start his own war. And he killed those who mentioned the name of Jesus Christ, while he also took upon himself attributes of believers, and he forgot what the Lord God Almighty had sent him to do: to establish His righteousness and His son, Jesus Christ, on earth. This Muhammad was carried away with evil, and he yearned for his name to be exalted. And his members were left with the memory of what he taught them in seasons and times of the Lord God Almighty, and they made themselves a kingdom that fought that of the ten kings. They will never understand, until Jesus Christ returns to part the living from the dead. And from that, Muslims who know the truth of the Almighty without regarding the requirement of their religion are the true witnesses to this idea similar to the believers of Jesus Christ, who were taught the *righteous way of Jesus Christ* from the time of the apostles.

CHAPTER 5

REAL ACCOUNTS OF THE SEASONS

This is the way the Lord arranged times and dates of the ancient world. Read Genesis 1:3–5. Then Almighty God chose to separate days into two, light and darkness, to be two different times. Light was to be the time of day and darkness the time of night. This is where the days began. In Genesis 1:6–10, Almighty God teaches us how He divided the heavens and the earth, which is in the middle, and hell below. There above the sky is water that sits on snow in the heavens. There is a great openness between the earth and the expanse of the heavens, as there is a great openness between the ground and lower atmosphere, which is hell. Also underground, there is water slowed down by the atmosphere. After that, there is a great openness, and then there is the lower sky. Below it, there is water as well. Here it became the day *following* the day of *spreading*.

In Genesis 1:14–18, we read that Almighty God has put here the sun and the moon and stars on the firmament of the heavens to separate the day and night and day to show the hour, day, week, month, and year. This is a day of shining. The sun is the great light that He has placed to rule the day. And the day begins at dawn. After the darkness of the night, there is a light that appears when there is morning. Seasons begin with the spiritual first hour, which is dawn. For today, it is 4:45 a.m. in the distortions of those kings and their gods. The hour of 4:45 a.m. is the correct first hour of the day and is supposed to be 1:00 a.m. in the morning. It is different from the one assigned by the kings of the world as 1:00 a.m. (1h00). It is equal to the first hour in the morning for language translation. There are seven hours in the night. Also, the first hour in the morning, which is fourth hour of the day in the spiritual consideration, they compare with their 7:00 a.m., saying it is 07h00 and that they were taught by men to call the first hour in the morning, even though it is false just because they had to satisfy the account of their spiritual boss to maintain the worship of their gods. See what the Bible tells you in Mark 15:25 and Acts 2:15. It says the ninth hour is the same as 03h00. That is certain, for they have not said 09h00, which today they refer to as the ninth hour in the morning. In the English language translation of this verse, we see if these statements are the third hours. And once again, Matthew 27:45–46 hints at the sixth hour of the day and ninth hour of the day. They say they are "6eme Heures" and "9eme Heures" in French.

These hours are very different from 12:00 and also 15:00 or evening, as the expression will also be at twelve and fifteen hours respectively in language translation differences and distortions in the Bible. Look at the count for each time. The difference in characters (digits) is six in order to spread their gods to get stronger. For example, their first hour is to be called 7:00 a.m. The difference is six. Moreover, they put the time of death as 00:00 hour. That is the silence of death, or there is no ruler for these times. That time, they made it to worship the gods and to prepare themselves to do the evil of murders, astral projections (Uwangaji), invocations (manuwizi), shedding blood, and so on.

SPIRITUAL MATH OF SPACE AND TIME

Hours of the Day	Human Order	Spiritual Order	Spiritual Gates	Our Time (Hour)	Angels' Timing	Elected Timing	Biblical
1st H Day	1st H	4:45 a.m.	1st Gate	5	Morning	Y1	Day
2nd H	2	5:45 a.m.		6		Morning	
3rd H	3	6:45 a.m.		7	X1		
4th H	4	7:45 a.m.	2nd Gate	8		Y1	
5th H	5	8:45 a.m.		9			
6th H	6	9:45 a.m.		10	X1		
7th H	7	10:45 a.m.	3rd Gate	11		Y2	
8th H	8	11:45a.m.		12		Day	
9th H	9	12:45 p.m.		13= 1p.m.	X2		

10th H	10	01:45 p.m.	4th Gate	14= 2p.m.	Day	Y2	
11TH H	11	02;45p.m.		15= 3p.m.			
12th H	12	03:45p.m.		16= 4p.m.	X2		
1st H Night	13	04:45 p.m.	5th Gate	17= 5p.m.		Y3	Night
2nd H	14	05:45 p.m.		18= 6p.m.		Evening	
3rd H	15	06:45 p.m.		19= 7p.m.	X2		
4th H	16	07:45 p.m.	6th Gate	20= 8p.m.		Y3	
5th H	17	08:45 p.m.		21= 9p.m.			
6th H	18	09:45p.m.		22=10p.m.	X3		
7th H	19	10:45 p.m.	7th Gate	23=11p.m.	Night	Y4	
8th H	20	11:45p.m.		24=00a.m.		Night	
9th H	21	00:45a.m.		1	X3		
10th H	22	01:45 a.m.	8th Gate	2			
11th H	23	02:45a.m.		3			
12th H	24th H	03:45 a.m.		4	X3		

The hour of 4:45 is the first hour according to the real time, the spiritual timing, the original time.

Timing and times are the secrets and mystery of God. This is the one that makes such a senior world weep (Acts 1:7; Genesis 1:14, 8:22).

Europe		America		Africa		Remarks
French	Hours	English	Times	Central	Timing Season	Observation
00 (24)	(Midnight)	12	a.m.	6	Midnight	When you research, you will find that English timing makes a difference with the timing of Central Africa. Places are marked case (6) also, in European hours, (12), meaning 6 double is indicating that earth is ruled by Satan.
1	H	1	a.m.	7	Night	
2	H	2	a.m.	8	Night	
3	H	3	a.m.	9	Night	
4	H	4	a.m.	10 (John 20:1)	Early Morning (Dawn)	
5	H	5	a.m.	11	Sunset	
6	H	6	a.m.	12	Morning	
7	H	7	a.m.	1	Morning	
8	H	8	a.m.	2 (Mark 15:25, Mt. 20:3)	Daylight	
9	H	9	a.m.	3 (Mt. 2:15–17)	Daylight	
10	H	10	a.m.	4	Daylight	
11	H	11	a.m.	5	Daylight	
12	H	12	p.m.	6 (Mt. 10:9, Yoh. 4:6)	Afternoon	
13	H	1	p.m.	7 (Yoh. 4:52)	Afternoon	
14	H	2	p.m.	8 (Luke 23:44; Mt. 20:5)	Afternoon	
15	H	3	p.m.	9 (Mt. 3:1; 10:30)	Afternoon	
16	H	4	p.m.	10 (John 1:39)	Evening	
17	H	5	p.m.	11 (Mt. 20:6,9)	Evening	
18	H	6	p.m.	12	Evening	
19	H	7	p.m.	1 (Luke 22:59)	Evening	
20	H	8	p.m.	2	Night	
21	H	9	p.m.	3 (Mt. 23:23)	Night	
22	H	10	p.m.	4	Night	
23	H	11	p.m.	5	Night	

NB: This Europa season is unknown in Bible plans (the word of God), but this African one is a clear indication that we have twelve hours of the day and twelve of night. John 11:9–10 is different from that of the English. It clearly shows how the people who signed the contracts with the devil changed the time and times to mislead the entire world into being controlled by the influence of Satan—for example, 1:00 in the morning (Franco-Anglais) is the seventh hour of the night in central Africa and 7:00 a.m. (Franco-Anglais) is the first morning hour in Central Africa.

KNOWLEDGE OF THE HOUR

NAMES OF DAYS OF THE WEEK

French	English	Arabic	Swahili	Blessed Names
1. Lundi	1. Monday	1. Djuma-tatu	1. Siku ya Kwanza	1. Anzia
2. Mardi	2. Tuesday	2. Djuma-nne	2. Siku ya Pili	2. Fuatia
3. Mercredi	3. Wednesday	3. Djuma-tano	3. Siku ya Tatu	3. Eneza
4. Jeudi	4. Thursday	4. Alhamis	4. Siku ya Ine	4. Angaza
5. Vendredi	5. Friday	5. Ijumaa	5. Siku ya Tano	5. Fungo
6. Samedi	6. Saturday	6. Djuma-mosi	6. Siku ya Posho (ya Sita)	6. Sathoni
7. Dimanche	7. Sunday	7. Djuma-pili	7. Siku ya Saba (ya Inga)	7. Sabato

Siwani: Esta 8:9

Katika hayo yote, kila wamoja wanayo siku yao kua walio itoa wakfu, kwa kumtukuza Mwenyezi Mungu.

- Roman-Catholic: Sunday (Dimanche)
- Adventists: Saturday
- Arabe: Ijumaa
- Tukufu Sabato
- Swahili: Siku ya Inga (saba)
- Adam called it Sabato.

We are authorized to reveal this hidden truth (Titus 1:3).

For the biblical approach to the way months were counted, see 1 Nyak 27:3–17.

We are discerning the knowledge of the hour (Luke 12:56, 21:24).

CHAPTER 6

NAMES OF MONTHS

The names of all these months of humanity are different and glorious. We will find that the difference between them is that the Arabic months as organized for their calendar are very different from those of the French, English, and Swahili speakers because they are under the authority of the Roman calendar. That is what has been leading the world from 321 to this day.

Even though the Arabs have been guided by their calendar, they have used it in the Islamic religion. But it's life, your business, and your time under the direction of the Roman calendar. In contrast to those of the elect of God, they are now given the responsibility of coming to make it clear to those who are hidden under the rule of Catholicism. Jesus Christ says this in Luke 12:2–3! And it is not only that which is hidden that is to be made clear, but there is much that the nations will know according to how we are led by the Lord God of Hosts, our Maker, by declaring this sacred work. Look at the comparison of the Roman calendar with this distinct difference.

French	English	Swahili	Arabic	Blessed/Holy	Verse
Janvier	January	Mwezi wa Kwanza	Abbib	Nisani	Neh. 2:1, Est. 3:7
Fevrier	February	Wa Pili	Ziv	Zivu	1 Waf. 6:1, 37
Mars	March	Wa Tatu	Sivan	Siwani	Est. 8:9
Avril	April	Wa Innee	Tamuz	Zantiko	2 Macabee 11:30
Mai	May	Wa Tano	Abi	Dioskuro	2 Mac. 11:21
Juin	June	Wa Sita	Elul	Eluli	Neh. 6:15

KNOWLEDGE OF THE HOUR

Juillet	July	Wa Saba	Etanim	Etanimu	1 Waf. 8:2
Aout	August	Wa Nane	Bul	Buli	1 Waf. 6:38
Septembre	September	Wa Kenda	Kisleu	Kislevu	1 Mac. 1:54; 4:52
Octobre	October	Wa Kumi	Thebeth	Tebethi	Est. 2:16
Novembre	November	Wa Kumi na Moja	Shebeth	Shebati	Zak. 1:7
Decembre	December	Wa Kumi Na Mbili	Adar	Adari/ Tenashara	Ezr. 6:15; Est. 3:7, 9:21

TIMING AND SEASONS

Roman			Holy Calendar			Bible
A Month	A Year	Research	Month	Year	Research	Scriptures
31 Days 30 Days 29 Days 28 Days	365 Days 366 Days	Year and months for this calendar climbing and decline.	30	360	Year and all months, it's parallel; 1290 days are the same and 43 months (3 ans and 7 mois); 1260 days are equivalent to 42 months (3 ans 1/2).	Year and all months, it's parallel; 1290 days are the same and 43 months (3 ans 7 mois); 1260 days are equivalent to 42 months (3 ans 1/2).

Timing of Men	12 hrs daylight / 12 night	Australia and America, Different
Timing by the Angels	8 hrs morning/day and 8 hrs evening and 8 hrs night	Australia–Africa
Timing by Elected	6 morning and 6 daytime 6 evening 6 night	Africa–America

CHAPTER 7

ADAM NAMED EACH DAY OF THE WEEK

See how Almighty God arranged them. They changed them daily for their value and removed three different days. They made the first spiritual day the fourth physically. All this is to displace the glorious things and place their evil so that it might prevail. It's better to give them the translation of the days of the kings of this world:

Anzia is the original name of the first day of the week in the Spirit. In Swahili, Anzia means "begin." The evil kings overturned it by calling it Jeudi or Jupiter, as its worth. Thursday, Thole, or Jupiter is a pagan god who rules the sea and streams of water, as well as bridges, rivers, and springs. He is involved in the destruction of mankind in the water and on the big bridge over the river. This one ruins the water and puts the poison of death in it. He is a versatile being of the waters and is associated with making friends with witchdoctors, soothsayers, and fetish priests to destroy people in water-related accidents and on the bridges or causeways. In the covenant with those they serve, they have decided to give him the name of the god of the ocean or fish god. Those who go to hell and who seek authority sacrifice their all in the water to get through because he is headquartered under the Mediterranean Sea. This one's wife is under the ocean abyss of Indiana (the Indian Ocean) and is called Krishna Dobir. Whenever you see an Indian idol of a woman who is surrounded by symbols of the dragon and has beautified herself so much, this is an image of Thole's wife. When you say "Jeudi," there is *jeu* "game" and *di* "announce." Here they mean announcing the game of death in the water. They share information about the murder, and it's a game to them.

FUATIA is the second day of the week. The evil kings turned it by calling it Vendredi, Friday, or Frigg. This is the goddess, Venus, the queen of Thole or Thor. She is a goddess worshipped as the god of the rainy season. Many pagans of northern Edoni and eastern Asia believe this. She is a traveler in the thunder in the car from one side to the other. She has power over all things in the air for weeks. This freedom is sufficient for a day for the pagans, and they organize a sacrifice and the sacrifice of blood for sexual intercourse and ejaculate sperm down on the ground openly and in using condoms. It is also the day the door of quarrelling opens, for the people have hatred and have personal jealousy, and through fornication, they break the word of the Lord God Almighty and activate the anger of the Almighty God from this word (Genesis 38:5–10). When you hear the word, there is *vendre*, a French word for selling (selling off), selling oneself, and *di* the French word for "declare." It means declaring to the people and nations that it is the beginning of the day to market oneself and do sexual intercourse with speed; sell one's soul, spirit, and body to drunkeness; and lose consciousness. That is the beginning of putting oneself in ignorance and distortions of the world since it is a free day for all.

ENEZA is the third day of the week, which the evil kings overturned and called Samedi, Saturday, Surtan, Star-day, or Saturn. It is the day the star performers uplift their female god by singing pagan songs, doing pagan theater performances, and presenting various academic showcases by professionals of magic (Magie) for their marriage ceremony in remembrance of them. They light up passions in the bodies of many and find opportunities for them to meet for cursed gatherings of pleasure. This star-day is the preparation for opening the door for Deus, their god, by destroying the Holy Sabbath, and certainly, they may become gods. Then this day is the Sabbath of the first material, which has already been destroyed. Surtan is the god of agriculture and has only civilization and uprightness of character. Saturday, or Samedi, has many sects that worship on this day, and others worship on their day of worship, which is Sunday. When you hear this day, you can understand these words: Samedi = Same-di. This means they have told me or I've been explained to. *Sa = yame me* means "oneself," and *di* means "declare" or "say." This means spread the day of all-stars or the stars of the world. Now you have been told about them through advertising on radio, TV, billboards, banners, posters, and even newspapers.

ANGAZA is the fourth day of the week. The evil kings overturned it by calling it Sunday, Dimanche, or Uranius. This is the god above all gods of the week. She has a word more powerful than even the wife of Lucifer, Monday. They make people do a lot together and are exhausting and governed by all the gods that gathered for the ceremony to tire humans for the first day of the week when Lucifer comes to control and organize the work of the week. All people are weak so that he is glorified by all people. They exalt him with their organs while they are bowed down, and its weight breaks them down with its burden, except those obedient to Jesus Christ and perfection in the way of truth and the glory of the Lord God Almighty. It is a special day to uplift the sun god, as it is called sun = sun, day = day. That is a sunny day. The day was specially planned to commemorate the work of the wicked to uplift the sun, who is the representative of the god Mithra, whom they worship on Christmas Day with Bacchus Dionysia. In Dimanche, you will find two words tied together: *dim* meaning "tenth" and *anche* or *anchor*. That is the light of the fire. That means that all the offerings are eaten and the tenth burned because it's all right. The sun is scorching light. The burnt offering is tithed or tenth now; it is not as a sacrifice to the Lord, of course not, but with pockets of wealth, pastors deny the poor, widows, and orphans.

FUNGO is the fifth day of the week, which the evil kings overturned and called Lundi, Monday, Lune, or Moon in English. There are other French words that relate to the Greek and Latin languages compatible in translation. All those ten kings brought them through these two languages: French and English. This Monday is the wife of Lucifer, a goddess who rules all the first day of the week, the day on which Lucifer abandoned his throne and came around to organize the work anew for his servants and his gods day after day, hour after hour, and called the timing of the week as a week. To the year were added six additional days. And then for each region and within each country and district, they sent a wind of laziness and human weakness that weighs them down with its great weight. While other creatures worship this goddess and offer gifts so that she can continue to come down under her husband, pagans and the darkness shed the blood of their children in the new moon to rule the devil and in the blindness of darkness. For this goddess receives worship each new moon and when the moon becomes full (Psalm 106:35–39). It's a union of two names, where there is a moon, its interpretation is as a radiant moon night and day. When you hear this day, there is the word *Lundi*, clearly indicating lune "moon" and di "declare." They saw it well to put it in the mystery of lun-di.

SATHONI is the sixth day of the week, which the evil kings overturned and called Mardi, Tuesday, Tiw, or Mars. Mars is a god of war, the high priest who has come to a band of the warrior Beelzebub, possessed by the god Mars. He also possesses this day to overcome conflict through humans and their living conditions in the corruption they live with each day of the week. On this day, there is a word *Mardi*, which indicates *mar* "jealous" and *di* "declare." It declares the day of jealousy, hatred, and sectarianism. Look through and you will see what day people do not get along and do not listen to each other often throughout the week.

SABATO is the day of rest for the Lord in the week. It's a glorious day. The evil kings overturned it by calling it Mercredi, Wednesday, or Mercure. It's a god-king of authority and leadership of the pagan who is given power and authority from the god Augustine so that the rule of darkness may spread throughout the world in every week and month and year. There is something in the word *Mercredi*. It shows *mer* "sea," *cre* "detail" or source of the hole, and *di* "declare." This day is a transparent declaration of the reign of darkness and hell. The word *week* comes from the English language, which is a week. It has the sense of depth in the mystery of the Spirit, as in "be famous" or "crow," meaning to complain or to declare the distortions of the day, month, and year so that no success is found. When you say the weekend, that is famous and take praise for yourself to the end of the week. Spoil your money and not have development in your success. Use foolishness and be ridiculous in the use of your earnings. Be praised by men yet be foolish enough to betray your Creator, and the heavens and the earth will one day laugh at you. There, you spend all the days in stupidity, worshipping all the gods of the week, month, and year. You will live in blindness even though your eyes are open. Then each day, month, and year was to be named after their kings and their gods so that they may worship from the beginning of the year until the end of the year. From the beginning of the month until the end of the week, its beginning until its end. And the gods are called saints. And many believers who have no godly knowledge are using the names of their children growing up. That is why you find most in the world are increasingly sinking into the mud pit of eternal woe, as they walked away from God and followed the gods of their fathers. These are their gods, whose names they bestowed on the months, and they are called the twelve heroic apostles of Satan. He has seven high priests to whom he has given dominion of the seven days of the week. Despite these kings of the world changing names and removing their worth, Almighty God has divine names, which He gave for months in His glory. We are going in this value of this day, since, in years, every month exceedingly loses its position. In the Spirit, today we are on the fifth month, which is Dioskuro, though in the body, we are still in the first month, which is January or Janvier.

CHAPTER 8

ORIGINAL NAMES OF
THE MONTHS

THE FIRST MONTH

Almighty God created the first month, and Adam called it **NISANI** in the Spirit when he was led to name things. It is Abib for the Arabs of Islam as revealed to Muhammad (Read Esther 3:7). But the kings of the earth turned it to Janvier, January, or Janus. It has thirty-one days of worship in it. This is the pagan god worshipped who opened the doors of the year that are output and success. He is called the god of the beginning of the year. He takes all the world's income, including from farming and agriculture, for mankind to begin the year with emptiness. All assets go back to him. And the angels of the state of their dark souls are engaged in helping to put the making cost of men showing off that they have no value or savings at that time. Conscience is disappearing, and the spirit says, "Let us eat and drink as we see in the New Year." People forget to prepare their hearts for the coming of Jesus Christ and are celebrating their shortage of days living in the world and going toward death. He has two faces, one in front and another behind. He has been worshipped since time immemorial, and even today, all nations worship in the ceremonies of the kings of the world and governments in the days of the month. At the beginning of the year, all nations give an offering from their property, alcohol, blood, through battles and killing, each by shooting and magic, poisoning and witchcraft. And on this day, the (New Year), there are accidents that happen. They lay their seeds in the way of immorality and pour it down. They also reward themselves for altar offerings and sacrifices of the blood of animals and their children, since the end of even last year to this day. Later come suffering and crying in hardship for all nations. Within fifteen to twenty days, people are hungry. Then he delights in this worship and the suffering of mankind. Moreover, every man declares in himself saying, "Thank you. I finished the year," even though it is self-sacrifice of jewelry bonds every year. They agree that the servants of the devil for one day transcend quicker than others.

The key for every day is to offer thanks to Almighty God without viewing day or month or year of birth. For example, whoever is born on February 29 can celebrate the great day of his or her birth how many times in ten years? For this day of that month comes once after three years.

THE SECOND MONTH

Almighty God created the second month, and Adam called it ZIVU in the Spirit, when he was directed to name objects. Ziv for Muslim Arabs was revealed by Muhammad (Read 1 Kings 6:1). But the kings of the world changed it. They were led by their master, Satan. They called it Février, February, Februus, Fanny, or Faunus. She is a goddess, the wife of Janus or January. This is worshipped in twenty-eight days in B and C in the Catholic liturgy and in A and twenty-nine in the liturgy of the Catholic church of the great kings of the world. Even though all denominations can insult them and speak ill, they are still under their rule because they are the ones who give the calendar for the program every year, and they are the ones who give permission to strike any country to famine and war. Each month, they're second in their honor to this goddess who is a farce (statue), rendering honor and worship tirelessly. This one is not worshipped for thirty or thirty-one days because she enters her menses (menstruation) for three days. That's why it was cut, to allow women to have sex for three days of their menses rather than the seven days that He commanded. Almighty God is the god of purification by means of pagans also equal to one another, their husbands and wives, for their wild animals and domesticated ones. He is given dominion over all creatures going to hell still alive from the hands of Satan. And he assents to allow believers to get property and income from sacrificing the concessions or sacrifices every year. She is the queen of the heavens, whom they give the position of Virgin Mary, mother of Jesus Christ. Another name is Marie Valencia. Its headquarters are in France. Then they offer incense and reinforcements for the application of power to that name. Remember this prayer note in the rosary: "Greeting the queen of heaven, greeting you, very good mother ..." Get light through this reading of Jeremiah 7:17–18 and 44:16–18. Without this queen, those who worship her feel that they will not have a good life on earth, though it is utter foolishness.

THE THIRD MONTH

Almighty God created the third month, and Adam named it SIWANI in the Spirit. He was navigating to arrange the names. Sivan for Arab Muslims was revealed by Muhammad. (Read Esther 8:9.) But the kings of the earth changed it, led by their master, Satan. They called it Mars, March, or Marius. He is a heroic male god who fights in war. The name of the game is death. He is worshipped thirty-one days. And in all wars of mankind, whoever first asked for his support in the war got the victory. They also deliver their sacrifices to overcome war and bust the heads of the righteous without fault, as is their covenant. It is a living hell for the headquarters of the dragon. There, they persist in eating and drinking the blood of those who have been beheaded. He stands in every place of war in the world.

THE FOURTH MONTH

Almighty God created the fourth month, and Adam named it ZANTIKO in the Spirit when he was led to name things. Tammuz for Arab Muslims was revealed by Muhammad. (Read 2 Makabayo 11:30–35). But the kings of the world changed it. They were led by their master, Satan. They named it Avril, April, or Apriel. It is God who manages farms and plants in seasons open for more germination of flowers and plants. He engaged in helping to destroy and eat plants like a field if the field was that of a pagan or a weak Christian who did not agree to make a covenant with the fetish priests to urge protection, molding the fields of those who did not submit to his hands. For those who do not know and worship him and who have no loyalty to the Lord of hosts, their plants lose their edge, and they weep bitterly. Many prayed for reconciliation and burned up cropland. This herb highly weakens their healthy humans, destroying them as it has formed in it. And, for a long time, it has brought diabetic diseases and cancer, hernias, and lung or kidney and intestinal decay. And that makes him happy. He is responsible for eliciting disappointment in humans, sending them in the wrong direction, in order to attract the world and forget their Creator. We must pray for our farms and agriculture to follow the criteria according to biblical leadership. God's Word says to plough for six years and in the seventh year not to plant anything. Do not plant two seeds in the same field; then at harvest, give a tenth of your field crops and first fruits to the Lord in the year so that He adds to your yields and protects your land.

THE FIFTH MONTH

Almighty God created the fifth month, and Adam called it **DIOSKURO** in the Spirit when he was directed to name objects. Abiil for Arab Muslims was revealed by Muhammad. (Read 2 Makabayo 11:21.) But the kings of the world changed it when they were led by their lord, Satan, and named it Mai, May, Arya, or Maia YHA. He is the god responsible for the chaos and raising the elements to do destruction and do it all the time—oceans, seas, rivers, volcanos, earthquakes, and wind—in moving the expanse of the sky from the east to the north. He is a gluttonous god who tirelessly eats meat from infant babies sprinkled with their blood and their oil so that he can take their stars and stay in a youthful state through the blood he drinks. And when he decides to do evil, he does it without examining any exemptions, friendly or royal, and bondage to anyone or anything. He always longs to have lots of good health in his body. He prevents disease spirits in this month so that sacrifices made then will be of good health until the month has passed.

KNOWLEDGE OF THE HOUR

THE SIXTH MONTH

Almighty God created the sixth month, and Adam called it ELULI in the Spirit when he was directed to name objects. Elul to the Muslim Arabs was revealed by Muhammad (Neh. 6:15) But the kings of the world changed it when they were led by their lord, Satan, to Juin, Jun, Juino, or Juno. She is a god who is believed to be the daughter of Juve (Jupiter), Dionysia, or Bacchus's father god, who is the only son of Jupiter, who was married to the daughter of Juno. She is the goddess of the Romans responsible for the women in their marriage and their menstrual days and also of contraception and children, so that humans should not bear too many but agree to enter into a curse in the eyes of the Lord. They were to offer to sacrifice their menstrual blood and infants in their pregnancy to her. She is also given backing by the world for common issues of marriage for men and women. Here, her name and her reputation have gone up so much for the devil because she has managed to conquer the world. Also, the devil has put her around him, as he has seen her methods are good in trapping them and bringing them under his feet. Then, woe in the world comes with great speed.

THE SEVENTH MONTH

Almighty God created the seventh month, and Adam named it ETANIMU in the Spirit when he was directed to name objects. Ethanim for Arab Muslims was revealed by Muhammad. (Read 1 Kings 8:2.) But the kings of the world changed it when they were led by their lord, Satan. They named it Juillet, July, or Julius. This is the god of the humanitarian Roman who does not die because his body has made accommodations with Satan to rule well and examine the continent of Europe. He called himself Nero Caesar. He is the one to whom they paid taxes from the era when King Jesus Christ was in the world, and even today, taxes are collected for him. It is customary for the kings of the earth, and all is accomplished and contributed through the UN and offerings in the Catholic church. He is capable of gravity in money matters and can keep the spirit of man to the level of killing and doing evil to get money or to face others and oppress them and shed their blood. Even for a single penny, he can grow your life.

Do not let the blood pour out. It's better to lose money. Money is not worth more than the life of man. This is also the owner by way of the hands of these precious kings of all precious stones and metals, such as gold, silver, diamonds, and the like. Heave money to get value or lose value attributable to the sacrifice that some countries offered to this Caesar Nero god who has carried the position of the statue. He has grown it and was designed as Nebuchadnezzar and his administration in the time of Daniel, a servant of God, and the era of pharaohs when the Lord came to the defense of Moses, who prayed for freedom from Egyptian bondage. The Lord to glorify Himself sent Israel into the wilderness. And this model was clear when one African king god who called himself eternal "Sese Seko," the cry of Mobutu, acquired all the assets of the country and grew its money in countries to bear the mark of its shape. That is the great curse of those to whom the disease will pass. All those who grew up on the land until the Lord God Almighty appointed the same king who will rule the three bad ones of Mobutu. And the king will grow to four, and three presidents will rule the land. The Lord will invent wars in the country blessed by those who lived in purification, for they shall inherit the earth tomorrow. These are the gods of money who are working around the world.

THE EIGHTH MONTH

Almighty God created the eighth month, and Adam called it **BULI** in the Spirit when he was directed to name objects. Bulliy for Arab Muslims was revealed by Muhammad. (Read 1 Kings 6:39.) But the kings of the world changed it when they were led by their lord, Satan, and named it Aout, August, or Augustino. He is a god who possessed the name of his father, Caesar Julius Nero, and was a human god in Rome. He has the relevant authority of chiefs and kings, the men who own this world. He has the human characteristics of businessmen, artists, football players, and musicians, and all are called to grow many stars of this world. They are given authority from this God, headquartered in China in Asia. All the qualities of beauty, art, and sports are also capable of leading and owning and have been given to him by the devil. He has appeared since the time of ancient heroes, as they made the decision to change the day and the seasons of the world. He gave them the conditions under which each king would rule the world. They must plan to stay with her contract. Today, many go through Americanism and Rome to the agreement since they are his delegates. These are mandated to inform him, and if it changes the Constitution, you'll find your president arrives and China is assigned to it and highly respected in hell.

THE NINTH MONTH

Almighty God created the ninth month, and Adam named it KISLEVU in the Spirit when he was directed to name objects. Kisleu for Arab Muslims was revealed by Muhammad. (Read 1 Makabayo 1:54.) But the kings of the world changed it when they were led by their lord, Satan, and named it Septembre, September, or Septy. It is the pagan deity who is concerned with summertime in Canada, Europe, and the United States. Pagans believed they could summon a god of sickness and disease with authority, framing and changing humans to grow the drug trade and extort sacrifice abruptly and mortality through different diseases. He destroyed the pagan way of witchcraft and magic, also put under the authority of the devil.

THE TENTH MONTH

Almighty God created the tenth month, and Adam named it TEBETHI in Spirit when he was directed to name objects. Thebeth for Arab Muslims was revealed by Muhammad. (Read Esther 2:16.) But the kings of the world changed it when they were led by their lord, Satan, and named it Octobre, October, or Octopus. He is god who rules in the water. He is called the master of cirène or god fish of the sea and a great big lake. The lake is *lac*, the ocean is the ocean, and the octopus is in the sea. This has eight tails and one head. Pagans do not believe in the god of water. He uncorks the waters and marine destruction, flooding the lake, and does not keep the aquatic harvests of their leaders. He guides the spirits of different animals and fish in their waters. The giant who lives in the sea, the sea, and the rivers also within the octopus. Marines who travel on all the trips to pay worship and render sacrifice compromise since the month of September to December is observed to be the high risk time in water transportation. The devil in return for their sacrifice receives for them through local waters. Africa provides these sacrifices, but after five to eight years, shipping companies in Europe, the United States, and Asia are where they spend their sacrifice, and the directions they give to the altar of the dark then start sinking emerging information, and their journey does not succeed again.

THE ELEVENTH MONTH

Almighty God created the eleventh month, and Adam called it SHEBATI in Spirit when he was directed to name objects. Shebeth for Arab Muslims was revealed by Muhammad. (Read 1 Makabayo 16:14.) But the kings of the world changed it when they were led by their lord, Satan, and named it Novembre, November, or Novea. He is the god of the pagans who manages rainfall averages and autumn, and they call him the fruit god. He is the one who multiplies and who draws the seasons' fruits and the trees to get fruit at home—apple, avocado, and the like with it. Sky has the ability to enact wishes because he has the biggest army. He is also able to curse trees so they yield no fruit. Pagans descended and burned, tampering with the faith of believers in Christ to twist and remove their confidence and consistency. He injects doubt, and they lose trust in Jesus Christ to show them that their application does not reach heaven. For those who are lukewarm, it is so. For those with firmness in Jesus Christ and who abstain from sin, it is different altogether. He is able to achieve aerial trips for travelers to get them through an accident. He still lacks one thing when we asked him to pray to the Father's hidden depths of our heart. Know of Daniel and Samuel, whose mother is Hannah (1 Samuel 1:12–13, Matthew 6:5–8).

THE TWELFTH MONTH

Almighty God created the twelfth month, and Adam called it ADARI in the Spirit when he was directed to name objects. They called the twelve, implying twelve. Adaar for Arab Muslims was revealed by Muhammad. (Read 2 Makabayo 15:36b.) But the kings of the world changed it when they were led by their lord, Satan, and named it Decembre, December, or

Decembius. This is the god who begins the season of cultivation and the god of ascent who grows able to install the luck and the grace of a man who is not within the blood of Jesus Christ and him that hath not been covered by the shadow of the glory of the Almighty God through the Holy Spirit. He has the power to deprive this life of lucky stars and give this to another pagan heathen. They are not capable of playing in output and the blessings of the faithful of Jesus Christ because they were liked by the military heroes from the Almighty God. This rule is also the god of the sky and magistrate of wild meat and so on. The names in the Spirit were real names of months and days of the week in the world. At the time, it seemed right for the mankind, and the earth yielded too much for his time. The Lord's blessing filled the country with the glory of God Almighty, which existed over the whole country (the whole world obeyed Almighty God and His Messiah).

When Jesus Christ was present in the world, they were no longer taught these names that are sacred to the Jewish and Greek language. And the use of these birds' names grew a blessing and success in both worlds and peace and comfort without any curses. When it was said, it was good, and human life became better and was more favorable. Because of the blessings, He has placed them within days of each name, Majid. And the light was declared and reigned with supreme peace through these names. But to grow, the devil was jealous, and much hatred and intrigue came to transplant other names full of evil and curses. And he had a desire to change the names of every day and the moon to rule mankind and to bring the curse of malice intended in these evil names of days and months. By day 6, the extra they had added, containing the bulk of the curse and vanity, also had betrayal unlike the program of the prophet of Almighty God. To this day, the seasons evolve and adjust so that humans can visit his left hand, which is six hundred and ten places and six (666). The way the months were changed, this January or Janvier is similar to that of the four spiritual ones, which is the month of Zanthiko (April spiritual). And the December of this day is that of Sivan. Now watch the destruction of the devil. All this power and blinding are given to children of God who have watched the Great Spirit. Since the kings, when they changed the names of the months and overturned normal times, it became a curse and cares for all creatures as the presence of the Lord vanished in the world.

The world remained empty after Jesus Christ ascended into heaven as the abomination of desolation entered the sanctuary of the Lord and the Holy Spirit left the church of the kujichanga and evil. Now watch the destruction of the devil, how he shared items for his bad tactics.

2019 AOUT | AUGUST

Jour	Lun	Mar	Mer	Jeu	Ven	Sam	Dim		Lun	Mar	Mer	Jeu	Ven	Sam	Dim
Date			1	2	3	4			5	6	7	8	9	10	11

Jour	Lun	Mar	Mer	Jeu	Ven	Sam	Dim		Lun	Mar	Mer	Jeu	Ven	Sam	Dim
Date	12	13	14	15	16	17	18		19	20	21	22	23	24	25

Jour	Lun	Mar	Mer	Jeu	Ven	Sam	Dim
Date	26	27	28	29	30	31	

2053 NISANI (1)

Siku	Fun	Sat	Sab	Anz	Fua	Ene	Ang		Fun	Sat	Sab	Anz	Fua	Ene	Ang
Tariki			1	2	3				4	5	6	7	8	9	10

Siku	Fun	Sat	Sab	Anz	Fua	Ene	Ang		Fun	Sat	Sab	Anz	Fua	Ene	Ang
Tariki	11	12	13	14	15	16	17		18	19	20	21	22	23	24

Siku	Fun	Sat	Sab	Anz	Fua	Ene	Ang
Tariki	25	26	27	28	29	30	

2019 SEPTEMBRE | SEPTEMBER

Jour	Lun	Mar	Mer	Jeu	Ven	Sam	Dim		Lun	Mar	Mer	Jeu	Ven	Sam	Dim
Date							1		2	3	4	5	6	7	8

Jour	Lun	Mar	Mer	Jeu	Ven	Sam	Dim		Lun	Mar	Mer	Jeu	Ven	Sam	Dim
Date	9	10	11	12	13	14	15		16	17	18	19	20	21	22

Jour	Lun	Mar	Mer	Jeu	Ven	Sam	Dim		Lun	Mar	Mer	Jeu	Ven	Sam	Dim
Date	23	24	25	26	27	28	29		30						

2053 ZIVU (2)

Siku	Fun	Sat	Sab	Anz	Fua	Ene	Ang		Fun	Sat	Sab	Anz	Fua	Ene	Ang
Tariki							1		2	3	4	5	6	7	8

Siku	Fun	Sat	Sab	Anz	Fua	Ene	Ang		Fun	Sat	Sab	Anz	Fua	Ene	Ang
Tariki	9	10	11	12	13	14	15		16	17	18	19	20	21	22

Siku	Fun	Sat	Sab	Anz	Fua	Ene	Ang		Fun	Sat	Sab	Anz	Fua	Ene	Ang
Tariki	23	24	25	26	27	28	29		30						

2019 OCTOBRE | OCTOBER

Jour	Lun	Mar	Mer	Jeu	Ven	Sam	Dim		Lun	Mar	Mer	Jeu	Ven	Sam	Dim
Date		1	2	3	4	5	6		7	8	9	10	11	12	13

Jour	Lun	Mar	Mer	Jeu	Ven	Sam	Dim		Lun	Mar	Mer	Jeu	Ven	Sam	Dim
Date	14	15	16	17	18	19	20		21	22	23	24	25	26	27

Jour	Lun	Mar	Mer	Jeu	Ven	Sam	Dim
Date	28	29	30	31			

2053 SIWANI (3)

Siku	Fun	Sat	Sab	Anz	Fua	Ene	Ang		Fun	Sat	Sab	Anz	Fua	Ene	Ang
Tariki		1	2	3	4	5	6		7	8	9	10	11	12	13

Siku	Fun	Sat	Sab	Anz	Fua	Ene	Ang		Fun	Sat	Sab	Anz	Fua	Ene	Ang
Tariki	14	15	16	17	18	19	20		21	22	23	24	25	26	27

Siku	Fun	Sat	Sab	Anz	Fua	Ene	Ang
Tariki	28	29	30				

2019 NOVEMBRE | NOVEMBER

Jour	Lun	Mar	Mer	Jeu	Ven	Sam	Dim		Lun	Mar	Mer	Jeu	Ven	Sam	Dim
Date					1	2	3		4	5	6	7	8	9	10

Jour	Lun	Mar	Mer	Jeu	Ven	Sam	Dim		Lun	Mar	Mer	Jeu	Ven	Sam	Dim
Date	11	12	13	14	15	16	17		18	19	20	21	22	23	24

Jour	Lun	Mar	Mer	Jeu	Ven	Sam	Dim
Date	25	26	27	28	29	30	

2053 ZANTHIKO (4)

Siku	Fun	Sat	Sab	Anz	Fua	Ene	Ang		Fun	Sat	Sab	Anz	Fua	Ene	Ang
Tariki				1	2	3	4		5	6	7	8	9	10	11

Siku	Fun	Sat	Sab	Anz	Fua	Ene	Ang		Fun	Sat	Sab	Anz	Fua	Ene	Ang
Tariki	12	13	14	15	16	17	18		19	20	21	22	23	24	25

Siku	Fun	Sat	Sab	Anz	Fua	Ene	Ang
Tariki	26	27	28	29	30		

2019 DECEMBRE | DECEMBER

Jour	Lun	Mar	Mer	Jeu	Ven	Sam	Dim		Lun	Mar	Mer	Jeu	Ven	Sam	Dim
Date							1		2	3	4	5	6	7	8

Jour	Lun	Mar	Mer	Jeu	Ven	Sam	Dim		Lun	Mar	Mer	Jeu	Ven	Sam	Dim
Date	9	10	11	12	13	14	15		16	17	18	19	20	21	22

Jour	Lun	Mar	Mer	Jeu	Ven	Sam	Dim		Lun	Mar	Mer	Jeu	Ven	Sam	Dim
Date	23	24	25	26	27	28	29		30	31					

2053 DIOSKURO (5)

Siku	Fun	Sat	Sab	Anz	Fua	Ene	Ang		Fun	Sat	Sab	Anz	Fua	Ene	Ang
Tariki						1	2		3	4	5	6	7	8	9

Siku	Fun	Sat	Sab	Anz	Fua	Ene	Ang		Fun	Sat	Sab	Anz	Fua	Ene	Ang
Tariki	10	11	12	13	14	15	16		17	18	19	20	21	22	23

Siku	Fun	Sat	Sab	Anz	Fua	Ene	Ang
Tariki	24	25	26	27	28	29	30

2019 JANVIER | JANUARY

Jour	Lun	Mar	Mer	Jeu	Ven	Sam	Dim		Lun	Mar	Mer	Jeu	Ven	Sam	Dim
Date	1	2	3	4	5	6			7	8	9	10	11	12	13

Jour	Lun	Mar	Mer	Jeu	Ven	Sam	Dim		Lun	Mar	Mer	Jeu	Ven	Sam	Dim
Date	14	15	16	17	18	19	20		21	22	23	24	25	26	27

Jour	Lun	Mar	Mer	Jeu	Ven	Sam	Dim
Date	28	29	30	31			

2052 ELULI (6)

Siku	Fun	Sat	Sab	Anz	Fua	Ene	Ang		Fun	Sat	Sab	Anz	Fua	Ene	Ang
Tariki					1	2	3		4	5	6	7	8	9	10

Siku	Fun	Sat	Sab	Anz	Fua	Ene	Ang		Fun	Sat	Sab	Anz	Fua	Ene	Ang
Tariki	11	12	13	14	15	16	17		18	19	20	21	22	23	24

Siku	Fun	Sat	Sab	Anz	Fua	Ene	Ang
Tariki	25	26	27	28	29	30	

2019 FEVRIER | FEBRUARY

Jour	Lun	Mar	Mer	Jeu	Ven	Sam	Dim		Lun	Mar	Mer	Jeu	Ven	Sam	Dim
Date					1	2	3		4	5	6	7	8	9	10

Jour	Lun	Mar	Mer	Jeu	Ven	Sam	Dim		Lun	Mar	Mer	Jeu	Ven	Sam	Dim
Date	11	12	13	14	15	16	17		18	19	20	21	22	23	24

Jour	Lun	Mar	Mer	Jeu	Ven	Sam	Dim
Date	25	26	27	28			

2052 ETANIMU (7)

Siku	Fun	Sat	Sab	Anz	Fua	Ene	Ang		Fun	Sat	Sab	Anz	Fua	Ene	Ang
Tariki							1		2	3	4	5	6	7	8

Siku	Fun	Sat	Sab	Anz	Fua	Ene	Ang		Fun	Sat	Sab	Anz	Fua	Ene	Ang
Tariki	9	10	11	12	13	14	15		16	17	18	19	20	21	22

Siku	Fun	Sat	Sab	Anz	Fua	Ene	Ang		Fun	Sat	Sab	Anz	Fua	Ene	Ang
Tariki	23	24	25	26	27	28	29		30						

2019   MARS | MARCH

Jour	Lun	Mar	Mer	Jeu	Ven	Sam	Dim
Date					1	2	3

	Lun	Mar	Mer	Jeu	Ven	Sam	Dim
	4	5	6	7	8	9	10

Jour	Lun	Mar	Mer	Jeu	Ven	Sam	Dim
Date	11	12	13	14	15	16	17

	Lun	Mar	Mer	Jeu	Ven	Sam	Dim
	18	19	20	21	22	23	24

Jour	Lun	Mar	Mer	Jeu	Ven	Sam	Dim
Date	25	26	27	28	29	30	31

2052   BULI (8)

Siku	Fun	Sat	Sab	Anz	Fua	Ene	Ang
Tariki		1	2	3	4	5	6

	Fun	Sat	Sab	Anz	Fua	Ene	Ang
	7	8	9	10	11	12	13

Siku	Fun	Sat	Sab	Anz	Fua	Ene	Ang
Tariki	14	15	16	17	18	19	20

	Fun	Sat	Sab	Anz	Fua	Ene	Ang
	21	22	23	24	25	26	27

Siku	Fun	Sat	Sab	Anz	Fua	Ene	Ang
Tariki	28	29	30				

2019 AVRIL | APRIL

Jour	Lun	Mar	Mer	Jeu	Ven	Sam	Dim		Lun	Mar	Mer	Jeu	Ven	Sam	Dim
Date	1	2	3	4	5	6	7		8	9	10	11	12	13	14

Jour	Lun	Mar	Mer	Jeu	Ven	Sam	Dim		Lun	Mar	Mer	Jeu	Ven	Sam	Dim
Date	15	16	17	18	19	20	21		22	23	24	25	26	27	28

Jour	Lun	Mar	Mer	Jeu	Ven	Sam	Dim
Date	29	30					

2052 KISLEVU (9)

Siku	Fun	Sat	Sab	Anz	Fua	Ene	Ang		Fun	Sat	Sab	Anz	Fua	Ene	Ang
Tariki			1	2	3	4			5	6	7	8	9	10	11

Siku	Fun	Sat	Sab	Anz	Fua	Ene	Ang		Fun	Sat	Sab	Anz	Fua	Ene	Ang
Tariki	12	13	14	15	16	17	18		19	20	21	22	23	24	25

Siku	Fun	Sat	Sab	Anz	Fua	Ene	Ang
Tariki	26	27	28	29	30		

2019   MAI | MAY

Jour	Lun	Mar	Mer	Jeu	Ven	Sam	Dim		Lun	Mar	Mer	Jeu	Ven	Sam	Dim
Date			1	2	3	4	5		6	7	8	9	10	11	12

Jour	Lun	Mar	Mer	Jeu	Ven	Sam	Dim		Lun	Mar	Mer	Jeu	Ven	Sam	Dim
Date	13	14	15	16	17	18	19		20	21	22	23	24	25	26

Jour	Lun	Mar	Mer	Jeu	Ven	Sam	Dim
Date	27	28	29	30	31		

2052   TEBETHI (10)

Siku	Fun	Sat	Sab	Anz	Fua	Ene	Ang		Fun	Sat	Sab	Anz	Fua	Ene	Ang
Tariki						1	2		3	4	5	6	7	8	9

Siku	Fun	Sat	Sab	Anz	Fua	Ene	Ang			Fun	Sat	Sab	Anz	Fua	Ene	Ang
Tariki	10	11	12	13	14	15	16	17			18	19	20	21	22	23

Siku	Fun	Sat	Sab	Anz	Fua	Ene	Ang
Tariki	24	25	26	27	28	29	30

2019   JUIN | JUNE

Jour	Lun	Mar	Mer	Jeu	Ven	Sam	Dim		Lun	Mar	Mer	Jeu	Ven	Sam	Dim
Date						1	2		3	4	5	6	7	8	9

Jour	Lun	Mar	Mer	Jeu	Ven	Sam	Dim		Lun	Mar	Mer	Jeu	Ven	Sam	Dim
Date	10	11	12	13	14	15	16		17	18	19	20	21	22	23

Jour	Lun	Mar	Mer	Jeu	Ven	Sam	Dim
Date	24	25	26	27	28	29	30

2052   SHEBATI (11)

Siku	Fun	Sat	Sab	Anz	Fua	Ene	Ang		Fun	Sat	Sab	Anz	Fua	Ene	Ang
Tariki	1	2	3	4	5	6	7		8	9	10	11	12	13	14

Siku	Fun	Sat	Sab	Anz	Fua	Ene	Ang		Fun	Sat	Sab	Anz	Fua	Ene	Ang
Tariki	15	16	17	18	19	20	21		22	23	24	25	26	27	28

Siku	Fun	Sat	Sab	Anz	Fua	Ene	Ang
Tariki	29	30					

2019   JUILLET | JULY

Jour	Lun	Mar	Mer	Jeu	Ven	Sam	Dim		Lun	Mar	Mer	Jeu	Ven	Sam	Dim
Date	1	2	3	4	5	6	7		8	9	10	11	12	13	14

Jour	Lun	Mar	Mer	Jeu	Ven	Sam	Dim		Lun	Mar	Mer	Jeu	Ven	Sam	Dim
Date	15	16	17	18	19	20	21		22	23	24	25	26	27	28

Jour	Lun	Mar	Mer	Jeu	Ven	Sam	Dim
Date	29	30	31				

2052   ADARI (12)

Siku	Fun	Sat	Sab	Anz	Fua	Ene	Ang		Fun	Sat	Sab	Anz	Fua	Ene	Ang
Tariki			1	2	3	4	5		6	7	8	9	10	11	12

Siku	Fun	Sat	Sab	Anz	Fua	Ene	Ang		Fun	Sat	Sab	Anz	Fua	Ene	Ang
Tariki	13	14	15	16	17	18	19		20	21	22	23	24	25	26

Siku	Fun	Sat	Sab	Anz	Fua	Ene	Ang
Tariki	27	28	29	30			

The peace of our Lord Jesus Christ, the love of God the Father, and the fellowship of believers in Jesus Christ matures among its members, and the Holy Spirit has dominion over and possesses your souls in trust and obedience to Jesus Christ the Redeemer, the Lamb who comes from the Father and who will come in time as the Lion of Judah to separate the living and the dead. Be blessed in Jesus Christ, who brought life to the world so that it could get salvation. Amen.

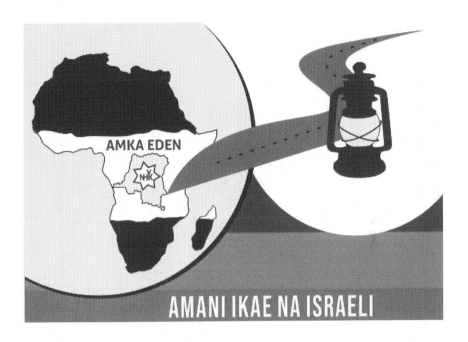

AMKA EDEN

AMANI IKAE NA ISRAELI

ABOUT THE AUTHOR

Torati is one of the refugee youth chosen by the God of Hosts. One day, in the second month of two thousand forty-two (2042), on our calendar, this was in the month of November 2007, in the refugee camp, the people were expressing their desire to know the Lord, our Creator. Life in the camp was so miserable. Angels of the Lord appeared to them and said, "May the grace of our Lord Jesus Christ be with you." They received it, and the angels stayed with them. They became friends of the Lord of Hosts. After 787 days had passed, the Lord sent His friends, and He returned to His heavenly dwelling. Then He said, "Go forth and follow the example that we taught you," but some were thirsty, and others were hungry. Then the Lord taught them again for a period of four hundred days. They came to know and understand many things, including the many secrets in the mystery of the Bible, which he made clear for their understanding. They were given the power to serve their fellow refugees by helping them with sugar, lamps, fuel for the lamps, and matchboxes; they shared candles and food with many of those in the camps. And the Lord has taught them to walk according to His will and not according to their wishes. And He gave them the work of proclaiming His advent through the True Way of Jesus Christ, which is their responsibility. They became enemies of all those who depended on the law and absolute doctrines of their denominations.

That camp is an example of the world that the Lord has given us victory over, as He has all things, because while there, many souls of the old prophets reached out to them and the Lord's archangels came to speak to them and encourage them.

Contact the author: torati@njiayahaki.org
Mailing address: 2212 67ᵗʰ Ave NE Tacoma, WA 98422

Printed in the United States
By Bookmasters